DISCARD

POEMS NEW AND SELECTED

JON SILKIN

Poems New and Selected

Jon Silkin

Muskingum

17. 4. 68

WESLEYAN UNIVERSITY PRESS

Middletown, Connecticut

Library of Congress Catalog Card Number: 66-14661
Manufactured in the United States of America
First edition

CONTENTS

POEMS NEW AND SELECTED

Brought Up With Grass

1

Brought up with grass,
Fastens under the doorstep, and catches
Between the toes. Not far off
A cut in the earth's moistened skin.
The fall's head disinters
A glutinous liquid congealed
Round air.

Many dismissive hands
Are like this dropped water.

Another gorge is close
Touched with the first's weakness—
This sheerness
A dizzying proliferation of dark, green moss
Dankening the acute
Corners of shafted stone.
At the bottom are ferns,
Spored and moist. The roof fell
Inwards, and over it gathering water
Moistens the dissident slab.

It is the water drops.
A man, occasionally.

Here also, a cave
Like half an eye in the ground:

The eye, out; its space, left
With falling into it
A jet of water that splays
Its energy, downward.
In and through which his father
Could be seen.

2

The tractor draws
The blade a foot's depth. The cut
Worm is writhing. This plot is deficient.
Inches food up the maize stub,
Into fibre matted with gruel
Of colourless nitrate.
The soil gives, he whispers.
Gives as it can.
A person, three of them
Sustained by its cumbersome wit.

The house shifts with wind
Inserted in ill-jointed planks.
More wood is in the forest
After cutting to be dragged
Off land wet with frogs' sounds.

It shall provide, he said.
Thrashed the grain. Small rocks
Gnash each other, who were one stone.
The wind has its heart.
We are more than stones; nature's produce
Choice, intellectual.
We adhere to her. The pine with swelled

Roots, a veined creeping
Over ground nutritiously furred
With needle's and bracken's tongues;
The split violet chewing
A knob of stone to grit.
The small wren bladed
With protective anger pierces
The intruder on the moss.
These are our fatherless
Coercive elements. Give us enough
To eat. The frost chars
The fatness of lobed blossoms.
Their death is ours. Our daughter
Sickens. I want her thick
Veined fat round the flesh, firm.
I want her speech to sieve
Into my breasts panicking milk. I desire
Her sounds over my face.

3

Nature pours onto the
House a burnished, lucid rain
That sieves through the palms
Of Hemlock.
There is no rationality
In her giving; breaks
Up or nurtures. I want moisture
For the ribbed palate; on the skin, warmth
Where the frost teethed itself.
I want consistency.

The wind desires lebensraum,
A small stretch of causeway on
The obtruding texture of the earth.

The brilliant frost
Champs its minute teeth into the blossom;
For some months, its last delicacy.

The shark forced by
Bereaved fishers to take
A poisoned sea urchin—
For seven days that melts
Itself out of the gut.
A disintered spike works
Through the muscle.

4

I am an ingredient,
And expect the impersonal
Pressures on a thing
Trying to survive,
Among what seems malice, or is beneficence.

The stung asp with its
Acidic portion, persists with it,
Is a nail, a scratched pincer
Of my thinking. I am shaped
Crab wise; or as a fly
Infecting with vomit and
The orts of virus
A bit of carrion.
Tusk of rampant fish. Or whatever

I am I am, too,
Lens-like to
The skin's infection, its movement,
Transist into the meaning of
The configurated shift of burning wood.

I will work to survive
With what will work.

I cannot bear not to
See clearly.
                I qualify
Others by their concavities. I form that whole
Of creatures creeping together.
A bit of metaphor
A clear one

My thin, sharp bird's breast-bone
Faces upward, flanged and curved like a wheel's rim.
The bones divide the rain
That falls on them. I chide grass
Where it creeps. I ate green shoots,
Water, and slime. My faeces were black and acrid.
I came to the land's bit
Where chipped, whitish stone heaped.
Something occurred. My thought
Quietened over torn stone.
A human that had no wings
Pierced four inches of steel
Into me. I cried once,
Swelling the fabric of air, like a sail blown
Into by rigid wind, whose seams
Tighten, in each other's strain,
Snapping meticulous stitching—
My body blown into,
My cry entering the water
Alive there, eating itself

Snow Drop

The blanched melted snows
Fill the plant's stem, a capillary
Of heightened moisture. Air weights
Round a white head hanging
Above granuled earth.
There, are three scarab-like petals,
Open, an insect's carapace
With a creature in these, poised.
It does not move. A white
Cylinder with two
Thin bands of green, broken
Away where that part finishes.
There is no more.
The sun's heat reaches the flower
Of the snowdrop.

Meetings

I walked from the town in
Mid-morning, by path that
Pierced the exhaustion of wheat.
Stone and glass lowered beneath
What I climbed. Its blue haze
Gave out, and the path sharply
Cut into blackish earth. Trees began,
Raising branches, their leaves
Touched with stiffness, hale though.
One with thicker leaf and trunk
Grew separately. I could not
See men at the back.
Another, I had not seen,
Turned through the gate before
Me, moving the iron through
Its railed arc, and he left
His hand clasped over the top
Bar as he moved it on.
     It was not gentleness
Nor age, entirely.
And after he was through
He pushed the quartered metal
Back on its arc, which shook.
I might have stopped, a pause
Of courtesy for age
But did not, and nearing him
He seemed to have forced his
Stooped walk to my side quicker
Than I to his.
     'This is the way into
The town.' 'Yes' I answered.
The question seemed to shake

His flesh; as if the voice
Of intellect were firm
Even in shrunk frame; smiling slightly,
As if the thought of his
Expended shape contracted
Mine in his. I asked
If he had eaten. 'Yes'
He said, crossing
His hands across his stomach to harden
His curved shape. Some earned
Hoard of thought nourished him.
     'Across that field my strength dwindled.
I took from the earth my frame's
Energy, tended one, with the other's.
I am this now.' I noticed then
His eyelids were too small
To cover the stiffened muscular
Sight. Came close to me,
Lifting his face to mine,
Elaborately spat onto
My mouth a thin milkiness.
     I would have hit him.
Some self-tenderness in
His body prevented me.
He slowly moved on top of
Grass trodden into earth.
From that tree he passed
I heard a core of voices
Casually bent
On profitless violence.

A Death to Us

A tiny fly fell down on my page
Shivered, lay down, and died on my page.

I threw his body onto the floor
That had laid its frail life next to mine.

His death then became an intrusion on
My action; he claimed himself as my victim.

His speck of body accused me there
Without an action, of his small brown death.

And I think now as I barely perceive him
That his purpose became in dying, a demand

For a murderer of his casual body.
So I must give his life a meaning

So I must carry his death about me
Like a large fly, like a large frail purpose.

Death of a Son

(who died in a mental hospital aged one)

Something has ceased to come along with me.
Something like a person: something very like one.
And there was no nobility in it
Or anything like that.

Something was there like a one year
Old house, dumb as stone. While the near buildings
Sang like birds and laughed
Understanding the pact

They were to have with silence. But he
Neither sang nor laughed. He did not bless silence
Like bread, with words.
He did not forsake silence.

But rather, like a house in mourning
Kept the eye turned in to watch the silence while
The other houses like birds
Sang around him.

And the breathing silence neither
Moved nor was still.

I have seen stones: I have seen brick
But this house was made up of neither bricks nor stone
But a house of flesh and blood
With flesh of stone

And bricks for blood. A house
Of stones and blood in breathing silence with the other

Birds singing crazy on its chimneys.
But this was silence,

This was something else, this was
Hearing and speaking though he was a house drawn
Into silence, this was
Something religious in his silence,

Something shining in his quiet,
This was different this was altogether something else:
Though he never spoke, this
Was something to do with death.

And then slowly the eye stopped looking
Inward. The silence rose and became still.
The look turned to the outer place and stopped,
With the birds still shrilling around him.
And as if he could speak

He turned over on his side with his one year
Red as a wound
He turned over as if he could be sorry for this
And out of his eyes two great tears rolled, like stones,
and he died.

A Space in the Air

The first day he had gone
I barely missed him. I was glad almost he had left
    Without a bark or flick of his tail,
      I was content he had slipped

Out into the world. I felt,
Without remarking, it was nearly a relief
    From his dirty habits. Then, the second
      Day I noticed the space

He left behind him. A hole
Cut out of the air. And I missed him suddenly,
    Missed him almost without knowing
      Why it was so. And I grew

Afraid he was dead, expecting death
As something I had grown used to. I was afraid
    The clumsy children in the street
      Had cut his tail off as

A souvenir of the living and
I did not know what to do. I grew afraid
    Somebody had hurt him. I called his name
      But the hole in the air remained.

I have grown accustomed to death
Lately. But his absence made me sad,

I do not know how he should do it
But his absence frightened me.

It was not only his death I feared,
Not only his but as if all of those
I loved, as if all those near me
Should suddenly go

Into the hole in the light
And disappear. As if all of them should go
Without barking, without speaking,
Without noticing me there

But go; and going as if
The instrument of pain were a casual thing
To suffer, as if they should suffer so,
Casually and without greatness,

Without purpose even. But just go.
I should be afraid to lose all those friends like this.
I should fear to lose those loves. But mostly
I should fear to lose you.

If you should go
Without affliction, but even so, I should fear
The rent you would make in the air
And the bare howling

Streaming after your naked hair.
I should feel your going down more than my going
down.

My own death I bear everyday
More or less

But your death would be something else,
Something else beyond me. It would not be
Your death or my death, love,
But our rose-linked dissolution.

So I feared his going,
His death, not our death, but a hint at our death. And
I shall always fear
The death of those we love as
The hint of your death, love.

Caring for Animals

I ask sometimes why these small animals
With bitter eyes, why we should care for them.

I question the sky, the serene blue water,
But it cannot say. It gives no answer.

And no answer releases in my head
A procession of grey shades patched and whimpering,

Dogs with clipped ears, wheezing cart horses
A fly without shadow and without thought.

Is it with these menaces to our vision
With this procession led by a man carrying wood

We must be concerned? The holy land, the rearing
Green island should be kindlier than this.

Yet the animals, our ghosts, need tending to.
Take in the whipped cat and the blinded owl;

Take up the man-trapped squirrel upon your shoulder.
Attend to the unnecessary beasts.

From growing mercy and a moderate love
Great love for the human animal occurs.

And your love grows. Your great love grows and
grows.

Furnished Lives

I have been walking today
Where the sour children of London's poor sleep
 Pressed close to the unfrosted glare,
Torment lying closed in tenement,
 Of the clay fire; I
Have watched their whispering souls fly straight to God:

 "O Lord, please give to us
A dinner-service, austere, yet gay: like snow
 When swans are on it; Bird,
Unfold your wings until like a white smile
 You fill this mid-white room."
I have balanced myself on the meagre Strand where

 Each man and woman turn,
On the deliberate hour of the cock
 As if two new risen souls,
Through the cragged landscape in each other's eyes.
 But where lover upon lover
Should meet—where sheet, and pillow, and eiderdown

 Should frolic, and crisp,
As dolphins on the stylized crown of the sea
 Their pale cerements lie.
They tread with chocolate souls and paper hands;
 They walk into that room
Your gay and daffodil smile has never seen;

Not to love's pleasant feast
They go, in the mutations of the night,
        But to their humiliations
Paled as a swan's dead feather scorched in the sun.
        I have been walking today
Among the newly paper-crowned, among those

        Whose casual, paper body
Is crushed between fate's fingers and the platter;
        But Sir, their perpetual fire
Was not stubbed out, folded on brass or stone
        Extinguished in the dark,
But burns with the drear dampness of cut flowers.

        I cannot hear their piped
Cry. These souls have no players. They have resigned
        The vivid performance of their world.
                And your world, Lord,
                Has now become
Like a dumb winter show, held in one room,

        Which must now reek of age
Before you have retouched its lips with such straight fire
        As through your stony earth
Burns with ferocious tears in the world's eyes:
Church-stone, door-knocker, and polished railway lines
        Move in their separate dumb way
                So why not these lives:
I ask you often, but you never say?

Death of a Bird

After those first days
When we had placed him in his iron cage
And made a space for him
From such

Outrageous cage of wire,
Long and shallow, where the sunlight fell
Through the air, onto him;
After

He had been fed for three days
Suddenly, in that sunlight before noon
He was dead with no
Pretence.

He did not say goodbye
He did not say thankyou, but he died then
Lying flat on the rigid
Wires

Of his cage, his gold
Beak shut tight, which once in hunger had
Opened as a trap
And then

Swiftly closed again,
Swallowing quickly what I had given him;
How can I say I am sorry
He died.

Seeing him lie there dead,
Death's friend with death, I was angry he

Had gone without pretext or warning,
     With no

     Suggestion first he should go,
Since I had fed him, then put wires round him
     Bade him hop across
          The bars of my hands.

     I asked him only that
He should desire his life. He had become
     Of us a black friend with
          A gold mouth

     Shrilly singing through
The heat. The labour of the black bird! I
     Cannot understand why
          He is dead.

I bury him familiarly.
His heritage is a small brown garden.
Something is added to the everlasting earth;
From my mind a space is taken away.

The Two Freedoms

There were two birds today
Broke from their cage and seemed as gold until
    In the dry sun, their bodies were
Transfigured; they hung like ghosts possessed with the silence
    But not with the shapelessness of
Spirits; they, in the sun flashed one gold flown

    Through another;
And then were quiet on the broad, trunked back
    Of the wood chair. They were
Inviolable, with that power and helplessness
    Which sculpture has. The sunlight
Smoked on them, gold were their wings, gold feet; gold
        sounds

    Fled from their throats quickened by
The winged sun that, for a moment, urged their flesh
    To the transubstantial freedom
Ghosts are. They in the sun became the one gold
    With him in dignity.
I caught and put them back into their cage.

    Surely, I thought, Man is
Ridiculous whose avarice for life
    Is that he must put life
Back in a cage, cage life; he will increase
    The flow of the cruel gland,
Then watch, then feel his power and its rage

    Grow and be satisfied.
I shut the cage door, I looked with a cold rage
    At their stretched screams of pain,

And I thought again of the stairs down which the world
    Turns from its prison to
The cage of the still prison; turns and is caged.

    And thought, but it is best
That they fly in their cage and do not learn
    Of that grey, ironic flight
From one space to another, but step down
    From their carriage in the air
To that humble, iron house. Safely the breast

    Has shed that gold
Which had perched, for an instant, on their flesh.
    But as these careful words
Turned in my mind, their cry like a stab pierced
    Me; I thought of my own
Wings, cut and trimmed by my grey God.

The Return

I have carried for five years
In me, your country cupped with oval leaves.
    It is a land quickened with streams
Which have no confluence, yet they now firmly flow
    One liquid star in my blood,
It is as a jewel there. It is fearful and

    Strange to attend you
For I once fled through your pattern, I who now cup
    Your shape in my palm, and I
Burst from the green veins of your delicate country
    Move into the grey
Borders of the town who crouches in her shadows.

    I revisit you now and find
There is nothing changed in you but myself, I am
    Like a bird
That lightly perches on the angular
    Chimneys of London; I see
The sour hands of that woman folded into her lap.

    And I divine I now shall
Not be admitted easily to your source.
    That image of your streams met in me—
As the confluence of the stars meets in the one eye—
    This I got when I saw
The white shoulder of your profound hill. You were

    Then simple to me, but my thought
That now so distorts you, helped by the sensual flesh
    That exudes its particular scent,
The scent that the flesh gives out, and the flowers exudes

As they are loved—the gesture
Of the heart and the movement of the flower are the same—

That starlike thought of you
Still treads through my head as a dream treads, quietly
And with precision,
Unendingly real because impossible,
That thought and that image of you
You now deny. I am refused by you.

There are a thousand stones in
The shallows of the Avon; must I tender these,
Become again the intimates of
Your intimates before I begin where
You started? The day's
Shadow has lengthened and the red sun stirring

Its recent beams, in the evening
Grinds up its heat still; in between the sheltering
Walls of the town
Where the poor's tears are dropped without the leaf
For their comfort,
The stalk for their pity, it pierces. May I attend

These stones, as tears should be
Tended. Say if you will admit me though
My image of you is false.
Then I can put my tenderness on stone.
I will become its friend
Who fold over and over the fragile white rounds
Of your demanding country.

The Coldness

Where the printing-works buttress a church
And the northern river like moss
Robes herself slowly through
The cold township of York,
More slowly than usual
For a cold, northern river,
You see the citizens
Indulging stately pleasures,
Like swans. But they seem cold.
Why have they been so punished;
In what do their sins consist now?
An assertion persistent
As a gross tumour, and the sense
Of such growth haunting
The flesh of York
Is that there has been
No synagogue since eleven ninety
When eight hundred Jews
Took each other's lives
To escape christian death
By christian hand; and the last
Took his own. The event
Has the frigid persistence of a growth
In the flesh. It is a fact
No other fact can be added to
Save that it was Easter, the time
When the dead christian God
Rose again. It is in this,

Perhaps, they are haunted; for the cold
Blood of victims is colder,
More staining, more corrosive
On the soul, than the blood of martyrs.
What consciousness is there of the cold
Heart, with its spaces?
For nothing penetrates
More than admitted absence.
The heart in warmth, even, cannot
Close its gaps. Absence of Jews
Through hatred, or indifference,
A gap they slip through, a conscience
That corrodes more deeply since it is
Forgotten — this deadens York.
Where are the stone-masons, the builders
Skilled in glass, strong first in wood;
Taut, flaxen plumbers with lengths of pipe,
Steel rules coiled in their palms;
The printers; canopy-makers —
Makers in the institution of marriage?
Their absence is endless, a socket
Where the jaw is protected neither
Through its tolerance for tooth,
Nor for blood. Either there is pain or no pain.
If they could feel; were there one
Among them with this kind
Of sensitivity that
Could touch the dignity,
Masonry of the cold
Northern face that falls
As you touch it, there might
Be some moving to

A northern expurgation.
All Europe is touched
With some of frigid York,
As York is now by Europe.

To My Friends

It does not matter she never knew
Who Pater was. What is rare
Despite the encirclements of marriage
Or even the political relationships
Affianced beyond parliament
Is love, which breaks the breads.
The staff of women, the dread,
The hunger of men, it is not
Just what I am capable of
If mature; it is the force
Behind those intimations of our senses
Progenitor to more growth,
If anything is. Remember,
The moulds of rock perish,
The flower so delicately formed
The minute exactness seems meant
To last. What does live
In the complex fabrics of air,
Uncoloured, and always nubile,
Is this man-like attribute.
So very carefully
Consider what you do
As an action related always
To this eternal motion
In man's leathery breast;
For the way we treat each other
In private is minutely
The way we deal with wives
And they their men. Even stones
Wrinkled in a contempt
Of their manipulators
Lie in some comradeship,

For their sakes. And for Man,
Men matter, whether that God
Who made us, and the stones,
Is watching us, or bored
With human agony
Lies in immortal sleep
Terribly locked, not witnessing
The outrages of human hunger
Bearable only because
They must be, even these uptorn
Grains of love that are burned
In complex and primitive agonies
In concentration camps.

The Centre

My ancestors made love
In the hot pastures of the near east
And got me my seed there.
I should be drawn to
The Mediterranean.
I suppose I am. Greece
Was the shudder of the bird from the high hills.
But Italy; those with gold teeth
Are plucked of these by the Italian;
His main industry is fools.
His landscape gathers on the surface,
Not deepening into
The scents of heat, that delicate
Strength which breaks through
The white, Greek rock
In veins of darkness
That smell of the mineral
Origins of men.
So there is Greece. But my mind stays
In a place I saw little of.
The river drifts through
The town, falling massively
Under a low bridge.
Geneva. Was it fixed
I should choose your cool streets
Hinted of by the south?
Round this place move
The ornate schisms, intertwined
And made fast by the vicious and costly
Emblem of puissant Europe.
Is it strong only? It is also
Absurd. It is a continent

Caught in its intellect
At which centre it drops
Into a great lake;
Like some bath with its plug out.
And it is here I am
Constrained by having both
Prevailing intensities
As locked, and as formed
As the coolness is formed here
In precision from the clash
Of oppositions. Such firmness
Seems pre-determined
And intertwined to a gap
That is the weave and the space
Made by Europe in struggle,
Where choice flickers, but does not choose.
It is where the tensions meet
And wear each other away.
The life of a great
Intelligent continent
Falls through the space
It has made in itself
With too much intellect.
Or was it the intellect
Sought for a bride
But found only itself
Sufficient for its appetites,—
Say a poison this chemist
Fatally delivered
And tasted, and decayed on.

Respectabilities

Many liberals don't just
Make love, they first ask each other·
And either is free to decline
What the other wishes;
That is, unmitigated
Possession of the beloved's flesh.
Nothing hasty, nothing unconsidered
Catches the liberal by
The hairs of lust. Nothing.
And this consideration
For those feelings
Of the approached one naked
In love or in hunger
Is extended to all.
He will, for instance, ask
A starving man if he
Would eat, pressing
For the particulars
Of hunger. And enquire
Why he is deficient
In bread. All men are treated
With such perception as stones
Get in subjection to
Their shaper, as their use fits
To his. Men are chosen to meet
That judged compassion which
A liberal has. A wounded man
Receives the ointments of love
From matrons, with respect.
Sex, the inhuman hunger,
Demands courteous
Submission, polite domination.

In fact, the turning world
A stone delicately
Veined with acceptable
Colours, deficient just because
Another stone has gouged
A bit from its flesh
Demands the liberal heart;
Though a different stone
Brutal in the untamed
Components — a misshapen
Tongue of useless rock —
Merits, and gets,
A frank dismissal.
And this, too, is fair;
Though more than half the earth
Is denied purchase on
That delicate conscience
Cash gives: a fair if privileged
Mind veined with gold.

The Wholeness

Tiny stones
Have misery
Unforfeited though bound with
Good roots.

The continual
Sway, deeply rooted,
Of the branches of solitudes
Shares pain.

Stones in
Their large or
Minute splendours, or the olive
That recalls

Its inner
Shape, even
The hand that planted it,
Bring little

To the flesh
With that
Spirit it nurses; we have
Small contact.

This olive,
With the hand
That scooped earth for it; masts of cedars
Poised high

In thought —
This sensuousness

This getting of images
    Was never

    Sensuousness,
But handled, merely;
I am a man waiting his dead wife's touch.
    And I wait

    As though
This getting of richness,
All unctions of spiced Asia,
    The animal

    Oozings of
Gums, salivas
Of odours that leaves yield
    To touching,

    Is nothing.
Truly this seems nothing
Compared to the modest touch
    Of the hand

    Gently
On cheeks, places
As curved, but laid modestly.
    We did not

    Share in this
Touching and yielding,
This courting sensuousness
    Of earth.

If then
I was content,
I should be glorious now.
    I partake

    Of the olive;
I plant and reap;
I have sharing in grinding of
    What I gather.

    Yet having
The harvest I
Do not possess it; it seems
    Its granary

    But not grain.
It is increase
But formally, mine as
    Stones are.

    I therefore
Distrust that past.
Many gathered seeds without issue.
    We walked

    You, the soul,
I, the flesh, speaking
As with finger-tips held up.
    And though we

    Have use
Of these, they

Are as if rented; no man's.
    And they

    Stand from
Their wholenesses;
We are two-selved
    Creatures that

    Each with
Self-violation charges
Under the strange, live sun
    Its destruction.

    The tiny stone
Of creation charges
The fluid in the crude oyster that forms
    The pearl. But

    No precious
Creation nor wholeness
Of charged pain beautifully
    Entire

Is of me; I have no commodity.

The infinite charges of the flesh
The commodities of sensuousness,
The olive, pearl, stones of creation —
In their sensuousness these tear us.

    Yet the mental
Forces billow, and joy,

If it is joy, as we are torn
    Quickens you to grow;

    Not as
A quick seed in stone
But as you never grew, swellings
    Of wheats,

    And then
The billowing of
The entire meadow of curved stem.
    Silent in

    The stirring
Crop, the predator
Is dismayed, and takes flight.
    I perceive

    Your growth,
In which
Perception plant my grain.
    For I

    Lived before
Through flesh only,
As it were, on some infinite store
    Of images;

    But on these
As the eye
Cannot touch and the hand touches,
    Merely.

As the seed
Struggles with
Soil to flower with assertions
    Of more seed:

We rear with
The one the other an
Infinite sensuousness of wheat
    In commodity.

The dying
Body in paroxysm
Turns over: we turn
    Away from

An older
Disaffection. The branches
Stir above the healed lovers.
    The huge halves

Of this life are one for once.

Depths

Textures. Why always textures?
The fuss. It is enough
You take and hold the thing:
That being warm it gives you
A special sense of permanence.
Since but for the whole shape
There would be no texture. Despair
Has texture. It is constructed
From a total helplessness.
Despair is texture; without it
We should not know how to face
The thing with such certainty
Of loss. But touching it
We very gently feel
The whole paralysis
Of agony give way
Into the steadfastnesses
Of reality,
The differing planes of surface
We cannot avoid contact with
Which employ the sunk depths.

Three Critics

I speak of three critics.
The first is the most considerable;
Yet for some time has been pre-occupied
With lineal purity,
Just as if syntax, that
Interlockage of human action,
Moved on the surface, merely,
Despite the medium.
His own verse is clenched
In morality, and cold
In the triumph of a voice
Supposedly neutral.
The second is one
Who asserts a belief
In the impersonal
In poetry, great poetry,
Suggesting the moral glimpse
Is suffused and obscured
By the insertion of
The 'I' in the text.
This can be so. He also
Wrote some verse.
The third still writes some.
He is like a ball
That lightly swerves, or even
In a high wind, is turned
By whoever blows, in contraries
Balancing all with civil
Hand. He has returned
Where he never came from.
This last, in some ways,
Is emblem of the first two,

Their stance cautioned
By the transparencies of intellect
Rather than intellect
Coupled to the embraces,
The convictions, of feeling.
And these three together
Composed in cold entablature
Reflect society which
Has little warmth, much arrogance,
And little firmness.

from NATURE WITH MAN

Defence
(For Ann)

What 'one-in-five' can do
No man can quite do

She arrived late, with this motto:
'Time used in reconnaissance
Is not time lost'. Useful hint
On how efficient our defences
Would be. Sent from the *Home Office*
On 'Work of some importance'.
And 'The first thing' she said
'Is that there will be four minutes
Of preparation before
The thing is dropped. You should
Instruct persons to stand
In the centre of what room
They like — for the blast,
Unlike the bombs of the previous war,
Will draw the walls out.
There will be no crushing
Of flesh. Instead
On all sides walls will reveal
The citizen unharmed.' Here a question,
But 'No' she said 'we have
From our *Intelligence*
Absolute assurance
Our capital is not targeted.'
Total warfare, by arrangement.
And she was sure, when pressed.
'But there will be devastation

As we now suspect, in radius
Of forty-four miles.
The water will be infected;
The light from the thing, astonishing;
Which though surprised by, we should
Not look at; but shelter
Behind some object "to reduce
Damage to the tissue"
From radiation; or shelter
Under brown paper;
Or, if you can, —
Sheets soaked in urine.

So women who crotchet, stop that;
Men labouring whose issue is
The two-handed house, set that aside.
Girls big and delicate
With child, turn on your side;
You will melt. The ravelling spider
And the scorpion whose prongs itch
Will fuse in a viscoid
Tar, black as a huge fly.
The whole of nature
Is a preying upon.
Let man, whose mind is large,
Legislate for
All passionate things,
All sensate things: the sensuous
Grass, whose speech is all
In its sharp, bending blade.
Leave not a leaf, a stone

That rested on the dead
To its own dissolution.

She left then,
As if she were with her feet
Turning an enormous,
If man-made, pearl
As means of locomotion.

The Child

Something that can be heard
Is a grasping of soft fingers
Behind that door.
Oh come in, please come in
And be seated.

It was hard to be sure,
Because for some time a creature
Had bitten at the wood.
But this was something else; a pure noise
Humanly shaped

That gently insists on
Being present. I am sure you are.
Look: the pots over the fire
On a shelf, just put;
So, and no other way,

Are as you have seen them; and you,
Being visible, make them no different.
No man nor thing shall take
Your place from you; so little,
You would think, to ask for.

I have not denied; you know that.
Do you? Do you see
How you are guttered
At a breath, a flicker from me?
Burn more then.

Move this way with me,
Over the stone. Here are

Your father's utensils on
The kitchen wall; cling
As I lead you.

It seems you have come without speech,
And flesh. If it be love
That moves with smallness through
These rooms, speak to me,
As you move.

You have not come with
Me, but burn on the stone.

If I could pick you up
If I could lift you;
Can a thing be weightless?
I have seen, when I did lift you

How your flesh was casually
Pressed in. You have come
Without bone, or blood.
Is that to be preferred?
A flesh without

Sinew, a bone that has
No hardness, and will not snap.
Hair with no spring; without
Juices, touching, or speech.
What are you?

Or rather, show me, since
You cannot speak, that you are real;

A proper effusion of air,
Not that I doubt, blown by a breath
Into my child;

As if you might grow on that vapour
To thought, or natural movement
That expresses, 'I know where I am.'
Yet that you are here,
I feel.

Though you are different.
The brain being touched lightly,
It was gone. Yet since you live,
As if you were not born,
Strangeness of strangeness, speak.

Or rather, touch my breath
With your breath, steadily
And breathe yourself into me.

The soft huge pulsing comes
And passes through my flesh
Out of my hearing.

Nature With Man

The lank summer grass
As it is, bent and wailing;
A scorching wind
Scours a whole plain of it.
Dust still oppresses. Then
As if the earth received
A bruise a pool of brown
Slime erupts slowly
From among the stems. Summer mud . . .
Hot and stagnant. The grass stalks
Stand pricked without root
In the rimless mud . . . in what eye.
On some field of grey stone
A white sud of saliva,
So fine it seems a mildew,
Agonizes over the crop.

But are the humans here? Nature
Had a human head. The mouth
Turned on its long neck, biting through
Scale, sinew; and the blood
Carried through the flesh
Beyond the ends of veins
As the severed head
Rolled into the bullrushes.
This limp and useless
Going off among tall weeds
Has soured the earth, whose body
Decays and perishes.
As for the pain
That suds onto the stone;
That, simply, is pain.

How much else is there?
There is only one head.
But it has several minds
Which still give out
Great reticulations
Of ideas, nets wilful and sharp
Over it; binding it
In pride and thought that cut
The smiling face of pleasure.

"O pity, pity, pity"?
But the weedy soul is shrinking.
Nor can it see how
To join itself unto
The membered flesh. The whole
Of nature is turning slowly
Into an eye that searches
For its most developed
And treacherous creature, man.
Monstrous and huge eye:
The entire process
Of nature perverted
Into the search for him.

A Kind of Nature

To Leonard Clark
For Leslie Norris

Keats' vision of Langstone:
Land and sea separate,
The first, sorts of mist. Sea fumes
Through a ship in sails
Coming thinly on.
The land fumes; so it seems
It too sifts through the ship.
Men's made things, images of them,
Replace what we have learnt
Of trees that hold the soil,
Or flowers, seen closely.
Their beauty still remains.
Not nature's, but the eye's,
Whose ligaments and moisture
Contain flowers that were flowers
Seen often. Oils of seed
In liquid chain held in
The lemon's crystalled sharpness
And green pulps of simple cabbage.
Great England. O what laughter
Of water ripples into your vegetables,
Or slender sweetness through blades,
The delicate grasses of sensibility
Purple, pale violet, or lilac,
The three-leafed clovers
Spread into curtseying
Demurely nubile.
Take care of Nature. Keats'
Vision must stay: a trope
For critics, merchandise

For types of shopkeeper
And poet; and be the sacredness
We use in churches
To justify 'the benign vision'
Of an indifferent God
Swollen with pulps of man.
He is our carnivore
And we, His feeling plants.
And that's the complex part.
For if He cared more
We might, like children
Put on trust, treat one
Another with more care.
For the price of having the Father
Would be obedience;
His images, our flesh.
But if we are alone
Like stones in a huge field
Stupidly brutal,
Where is the trust, that fine
Sharpness of moral care
Pervading each recess
Of lemon consciousness?
Nothing will guide
The pressed stones open
To the waters of heaven
That erode us, as we nudge
Wear and crack each other;
Though we are a beauteous
Gift of each other.

Dandelion

Slugs nestle where the stem
Broken, bleeds milk.
The flower is eyeless: the sight is compelled
By small, coarse, sharp petals,
Like metal shreds. Formed,
They puncture, irregularly perforate
Their yellow, brutal glare.
And certainly want to
Devour the earth. With an ample movement
They are a foot high, as you look.
And coming back, they take hold
On pert domestic strains.
Others' lives are theirs. Between them
And domesticity,
Grass. They infest its weak land;
Fatten, hide slugs, infestate.
They look like plates; more closely
Like the first tryings, the machines, of nature
Riveted into her, successful.

A Bluebell

Most of them in the first tryings
Of nature, hang at angles,
Like lamps. These though
Look round, like young birds,
Poised on their stems. Closer,
In all their sweetness, malevolent. For there is
In the closed, blue flower, gas-coloured,
A seed-like dark green eye.
Carraway, grained, supple,
And watching; it is always there,
Fibrous, alerted,
Coarse grained enough to print
Out all your false delight
In 'sweet nature'. This is struggle.
The beetle exudes rot: the bee
Grapples the reluctant nectar
Coy, suppurating, and unresigned.
Buds print the human passion
Pure now not still immersed
In fighting wire worms.

Lilies of the Valley

Minute flowers harden. Depend
From thin bowing stem;
Are white as babies' teeth.
With broad leaves, immobile;
Are sheath-like, and fat.
What have these to do with beauty?
They must take you with
A fingering odour, clutches the senses,
Fills the creases and tightens the wind's seams,
As noise does. The plant is equipped.
Even then you don't like it.
Gradually though
Its predatory scent
Betters you, forces you, and more than
The protected rose creating
A sculptured distant adulation
For itself. This insinuates, then grapples you,
Being hungry; not poised, not gerundive.
Hard, and uncrushed, these flowerheads;
Like beads, in your palm.
You cannot destroy that conquering amorousness
Drenches the glands, and starts
The belled memory. Glows there, with odour.
Memorable as the skin
Of a fierce animal.

Peonies

It has a group of flowers.
Its buds shut, they exude
A moisture, a gum, expressed
From the sepals' metallic pressures.
Its colour shows between shields,
Cramped where the long neck
Swells into the head. Then they open.
They do it gradually,
Stammer at first. It is a confidence
Permits this; push aside
The shield, spray outwards,
Mount in height and colour
Upon the stem.
They claim the attention, up there,
The focus of all else. Not aloof at all;
Brilliantly intimate,
They make the whites of others
A shrunk milk. They must draw
To them, the male ardours,
Enthusiasms; are predatory
In seeking them. Obliterate the garden
In flickerless ease, gouging out
The reluctant desires. Theirs is one rule,
And is found everywhere
Feeling transpires — extends
Its tendrils, helplessly grappling for
Passion of a different order
Than the peonies'.
What will be looked at,
However fleshily adequate,
Conquers the amorous.
By nature, a devourer. Cannot give.

Gives nothing.
In winter shrinks to a few sticks,
Its reversion, bunches of hollowness.
Pithless. Insensate, as before.

The Strawberry Plant

The rootless strawberry plant
Moves across the soil. It hops
Six inches. Has no single location,
Or root.
You cannot point to its origin,
Or parent. It shoots out
A pipe, and one more plant
Consolidates its ground.
It puts out crude petals, loosely met.
As if the business of flowering
Were to be got over. Their period is brief.
Even then, the fruit is green,
Swart, hairy. Its petals invite tearing
And are gone quickly,
As if they had been. The fruit swells,
Reddens, becomes succulent.
Propagation through the devouring
Appetite of another.
Is sweet, seeded, untruculent;
Slugs like it, all over.
It is nubile to the lips,
And survives even them. And teeth,
Insane with edible fury,
Of the loving kind.

A Daisy

Look unoriginal
Being numerous. They ask for attention
With that gradated yellow swelling
Of oily stamens. Petals focus them:
The eye-lashes grow wide.
Why should not one bring these to a funeral?
And at night, like children,
Without anxiety, their consciousness
Shut with white petals.

Blithe, individual.

The unwearying, small sunflower
Fills the grass
With versions of one eye.
A strength in the full look
Candid, solid, glad.
Domestic as milk.

In multitudes, wait,
Each, to be looked at, spoken to.
They do not wither;
Their going, a pressure
Of elate sympathy
Released from you.
Rich up to the last interval
With minute tubes of oil, pollen;
Utterly without scent, for the eye,
For the eye, simply. For the mind
And its invisible organ,
That feeling thing.

The Violet

The lobed petals receive
Each other's nestling shape.

We share the sun's beneficence:
Frost, men, snowdrops.
Then the violet unfolds. Not an uncasing
Of the corolla, each petal compliant
To the purpose of survival, obedient to that; but as it feels
The sun's heat, that puberty
Pushes out from its earlier self-clasping
Two distinct, clenched halves. Stiffens them.
These fluttering portions that made
The bud, separately elect
To be the flower; the violet
Halves itself, pushing apart
In two separate forces;
It divides up itself, it becomes two violet portions.
It is not a conformation of members,
Each petal a tooth, an eyelash.
On the other hand, the violet is torn apart.
Its increase is by dividing;
Its stiffened petals push further apart.
It adheres to its nature; it has no maturity,
Other than this.
It requires courage, and finds that
In this unclasping of its self-worship: two palms tentatively
Open. Going both ways,
They absorb a huge circle
Of violeted air, an intent
Movement of embrace;

Created, exposed, powerful.
The air is coloured somewhat violet.
It costs itself much.

Milkmaids (Lady's Smock)

Ridging the stalk's length,
The pith ducts. You'd think
The leaves found by water. Their openness
Guards them; a giddy, a careless
Effusion of stem. That is strength.
From the topmost, a flower triumphs.
From each undomestic
Flare, four petals; thrown wide; a flexible
Unplanned exuberance.
A veined fat is under
The svelte integument;
A kind of vegetative warmth.
From the centre, axial, determined
Extend the stamens, long by usage
For survival, and grouped
Round the curt stigma. Nothing less enslaved,
Less domestic to man, they are twice free.
Will wander through your plot in whole families.
You will not cut milkmaids down.

That tender, that wild, strength
Sucks the untrammelled consciousness up.
They mount the incline breathless
Pale violet. Their eyes wide,
They halt at the wire. This is the camp.
In silent shock a multitude of violet faces
Their aghast petals stiff, at the putresence
Of the crowd wired up. This halts them:
The showing bone; the ridges of famine,
Protrusions, want, reduction.
Silent also, they confront with their modesty
Of demeanour — the stiff fatigue

Of the sack jackets something altogether different
From those who supervise
In their soft, rigid cloth —
The prisoners confront
The unservanted faces of the plants.

Between their silences, comprehension; like the wire
Halted, staked, live.
Crowding through the tented cloth
That locust death, to each person.
For the flowers, the forked,
Upright sense of human
Creatures wanting patience, pulped, compounded
                                        into their children.

Moss

'Patents' will burn it out; it would lie there
Turning white. It shelters on the soil; quilts it.
So persons lie over it; but look closely:
The thick, short green threads quiver like an animal
As a fungoid quivers between that and vegetable:
A mushroom's flesh with the texture and consistency
                                          of a kidney.

Moss is soft as a pouch.
There are too many shoots though, boxed compacted,
Yet nestling together,
Softly luminous.
They squirm minutely. The less compact kind
Has struggling white flowers; closed,
Like a minute bell's clapper;
So minute that opened then, its stretch seems wide.
The first grows in damper places.
With what does it propagate?
Quiet, of course, it adheres to
The cracks of waste-pipes, velvets,
Velours them; an enriching
Unnatural ruff swathing the urban 'manifestation':
The urban nature is basemented, semi-dark;
It musts, it is alone.

Here moss cools; it has no children;
It amplifies itself.
Could that over-knit fiction of stubbed threads reproduce
Defined creatures?
It hovers tentatively between one life and another,
Being the closed-road of plants,
Its mule; spreads only its kind —

A soft stone. It is not mad.
Reared on the creeping dankness of earth
It overspreads, smears, begrudges something
Though it is passive; spreads wildly.
It is immune to nothing;
You cannot speak of misery to it.

Crowfoot (in water)

It is found, rooted,
In still water. A leaf,
Shaped like a kidney, floats
Leafing the underside of air, over water,
Taking in both, each side.
Inside the water
Are filaments of flesh-thread
Hair-drifting.
The flowers are white,
Simple, articulate.
Nothing smutches them.
Mouths of cattle, large
As sycamore trees,
Eat and compact stalk,
Leaf, stigma, and pigment
Into their food.

Shapes that no flower bred,
Not like any contour of nature,
Are piece-mealed
To a sponge of surging parts.

Articulate plant-speech does smutch
The ridged palate, bellying towards
The organ of hunger, minutely impotent.
The chopped articulation in the throat, —
Cattle's throat, — the woe
Is devoured. Crowfeet concerts
Its parts in a webbed cry.

If ripe, the seeds rear in
Dung casually dropped.

The rest persists under
The pond's rim. Can be devoured
To an inch of its life.

Small Celandine

Its petals close onto
A bland, contiguous sleep.
When open, they shoot from
That part large with organs,
Hips and face merged
In a thick, capable frame.
Its high crutched head is genitalled
For survival by display.
Flowers' conduct is supreme:
Fruit cankers, but petals age.
Insect life feeds on
Not it but its ripe seed,
Excreting over it; shard, rind, and succulence
Pinched by the sharp, smooth jaws.
A flower survives this. Small Celandine
Has sharp petals, its intensifying
Of their length, a self-absorption
That desires no further object.
Its lithe, green underside
Governs, with its greater thickness,
Each petal's direction. Leaves swaddle
The stem, as if near water.
It is indifferent to light, persisting with
Little sleep. It will
Not open or shut with what
Strikes into its senses.
It is insomniac
To that, merging it
With its form that presses little
Of itself on our minds.
We are not its leaf, its breathing.

Its adult, consciousless
Roots concert the sensuous
Nourishment of earth.

Goat's Beard and Daisy

They are closed, by noon,
Their petals held upwards.
In this sense, sleep is tension,
The closed tips of petals strained
Together, carefully.
If fertilized, they close earlier;
Conception achieved through
The stealth of a third. A plunderer
Covers the rooted creature's face.
The flower's silence is
Taken for deafness. As the insect hovers
Its passage is tautened through
Two kinds of organs' needs.
And what they have to give
Is as the bee nectars. Then they close.

The daisy has its mode.
It will close at night,
Or when rain gusts;
The soft, pouting stigma takes
The pungent, oily stamen's yielded pollen;
Grain is crammed in the gently
Insistent opening.
What the flower does it may do alone.
It will be beaten down, rather than open.
Rain squalls,
And sheets the swelling ground;
The closed daisy is fertilized.
When light comes, it responds,
Watching with one eye

A tree's bough
Wet all over, the antlered form
Stiff through girth, not pride.

THE WESLEYAN POETRY PROGRAM

Distinguished contemporary poetry in cloth and **paperback** *editions*

Alan Ansen:	*Disorderly Houses* (1961)
John Ashbery:	*The Tennis Court Oath* (1962)
Robert Bagg:	*Madonna of the Cello* (1961)
Robert Bly:	*Silence in the Snowy Fields* (1962)
Tram Combs:	*st. thomas. poems.* (1965)
Donald Davie:	*Events and Wisdoms* (1965)
Donald Davie:	*New and Selected Poems* (1961)
James Dickey:	*Buckdancer's Choice* (1965)
James Dickey:	*Drowning With Others* (1962)
James Dickey:	*Helmets* (1964)
David Ferry:	*On the Way to the Island* (1960)
Robert Francis:	*The Orb Weaver* (1960)
John Haines:	*Winter News* (1966)
Richard Howard:	*Quantities* (1962)
Barbara Howes:	*Light and Dark* (1959)
David Ignatow:	*Figures of the Human* (1964)
David Ignatow:	*Say Pardon* (1961)
Donald Justice:	*The Summer Anniversaries* (1960) (A Lamont Poetry Selection)
Chester Kallman:	*Absent and Present* (1963)
Vassar Miller:	*My Bones Being Wiser* (1963)
Vassar Miller:	*Wage War on Silence* (1960)
W. R. Moses:	*Identities* (1965)
Donald Petersen:	*The Spectral Boy* (1964)
Hyam Plutzik:	*Apples from Shinar* (1959)
Vern Rutsala:	*The Window* (1964)
Jon Silkin:	*Poems New and Selected* (1966)
Louis Simpson:	*At the End of the Open Road* (1963) (Pulitzer Prize in Poetry, 1964)
Louis Simpson:	*A Dream of Governors* (1959)
James Wright:	*The Branch Will Not Break* (1963)
James Wright:	*Saint Judas* (1959)